Proverbs
& Praise

Print ISBN 978-1-62416-128-5

eBook Editions:
Adobe Digital Edition (.epub) 978-1-62416-497-2
Kindle and MobiPocket Edition (.prc) 978-1-62416-496-5

Published by Barbour Publishing, Inc., P.O. Box 719, Uhrichsville, Ohio 44683, www.barbourbooks.com

Our mission is to publish and distribute inspirational products offering exceptional value and biblical encouragement to the masses.

Member of the
Evangelical Christian
Publishers Association

Printed in China.

MariLee Parrish

Prayers and Devotions for Women

Proverbs & Praise

BARBOUR
PUBLISHING

Contents

Introduction

Throughout this devotional book, we'll explore what the Psalms and Proverbs have to say about God—and how to apply that to our daily lives as women. Maybe you've walked with God for years or maybe you're just learning about God and want to know Him more. Either way, there is great wisdom to be found in these two books of the Bible. Everything from worship and work to family relationships and friendships, Psalms and Proverbs has something to say about it all!

Praying for you as we journey together,
MariLee Parrish
www.marileeparrish.com

What happens is that the almighty Creator, the Lord of hosts, the great God before whom the nations are as a drop in a bucket, comes to you and begins to talk to you through the words and truths of holy Scripture.

J. I. PACKER, *KNOWING GOD*

Knowing God: Wisdom for Life

The Beginning of Knowledge

*To know wisdom and instruction, to understand
words of insight, to receive instruction in wise dealing,
in righteousness, justice, and equity; to give prudence
to the simple, knowledge and discretion to the
youth—Let the wise hear and increase in learning,
and the one who understands obtain guidance. . . .
The fear of the Lord is the beginning of knowledge;
fools despise wisdom and instruction.*

PROVERBS 1:2–5, 7 ESV

The book of Proverbs tells us that fearing the Lord is the start of true knowledge. To fear God simply means that you recognize God's power and that you strive to follow His commands. It doesn't mean that you should fear that God is a grumpy old man, sitting at the edge of heaven waiting to "get" you or catch you in sin.

Getting to *know* God is much different than knowing facts *about* God. Many people could tell you the Gospel story from memory, rehearse all Ten Commandments, and explain steps to salvation and yet still not really know God personally.

Listen as God whispers truth to you through the books of Psalms and Proverbs. Get to know your Creator. He wants an intimate, moment-by-moment relationship with you.

As believers, we don't have to go through life on our own, constantly wondering which path to take or worrying over decisions past and future. God has equipped us with everything we need to live a godly life (2 Peter 1:3).

Stop worrying. Start knowing.

God Knows Me

You have searched me, Lord, and you know me.
You know when I sit and when I rise;
you perceive my thoughts from afar. You discern
my going out and my lying down; you are familiar
with all my ways. Before a word is on
my tongue you, Lord, know it completely.
PSALM 139:1–4 NIV

Many of us grew up with some sort of knowledge of God. Maybe your family went to church every Sunday, maybe your grandmother took you on occasion, or maybe you were a holiday-only churchgoer. Whatever the case, you probably grew up with some idea about God.

But did you realize that God actually knows YOU? Not just your family or the pastor at whatever church you may have attended—but He knows YOU! Personally. Intimately. The Bible tells us He knows how many hairs are on our heads. Before we say a word, He knows what it will be. He knows when we're going to sit down, stand up, go shopping, think a thought—everything!

Even if you've ignored God for a lifetime, He hasn't ignored you.

Open your Bible and read Psalm 139:1–16. Let it sink into your soul. Even though there are billions of people in this world, God made you and He cares about you. He knows your name. He loves you more than you could ever imagine.

Ask God to open your heart to His love so that you can be fully aware of Him.

God Made the Box

You hem me in behind and before, and you lay your hand upon me. Such knowledge is too wonderful for me, too lofty for me to attain.
PSALM 139:5–6 NIV

You might be thinking—*really?* How is it possible for God to care about my thoughts and feelings? With billions of people to watch over, how can He possibly know me?

When we limit our thinking to what we believe is possible, we put God in a box. God is the divine Creator. He made the box. The Bible says that such knowledge is too much for us to grasp. God is the God of the impossible (Luke 1:35–38). He is beyond the limitations of the human mind.

The truth is, He does know you. He does care. He loves you beyond what your mind can fully understand. He just does. It's a faith thing. Ephesians 3:20 tells us that God is able to do exceedingly, abundantly more than what we could ever ask or even think!

Caring about us personally is one of those things. Think about the heavens, the stars, the universe, the brilliant colors of the seasons, the intricate way the human body works. God is behind all of that. And yet the Bible tells us that He knows when a sparrow falls (Matthew 10:29)! And He cares more about us than anything else in all creation. How is that even possible? What is impossible to us is possible with God (Luke 18:27)!

Open up the box. Open up your heart. Ask God to strengthen your faith in Him. Ask Him to help you believe.

And even if you've walked with God your whole life, there is always room to grow in faith. To know Him more.

My Creator

*For you created my inmost being; you knit
me together in my mother's womb. I praise you
because I am fearfully and wonderfully made;
your works are wonderful, I know that full well.
My frame was not hidden from you when I was
made in the secret place, when I was woven together
in the depths of the earth. Your eyes saw my
unformed body; all the days ordained for
me were written in your book before
one of them came to be.*

PSALM 139:13–16 NIV

Not only is God the creator of the universe, He created *you*! In His image. And while He was forming your heart, the Bible tells us that He set eternity right there inside (Ecclesiastes 3:11). So as long as we live, we will never be made whole until we have made peace with our Creator— until we've accepted His love and begin to live out a daily relationship with Him.

God wants us to know Him. He's not playing games or hiding from us. He wants us to be fully aware that His power and presence are available to us as we go through every moment of life. He created us to have an eternal relationship with Him.

You don't have to wonder what God thinks about you. God has given you His Word that is full of living power (Hebrews 4:12). Did you catch that? God's Word is *living* and *active*! He tells you plainly how much He loves and cares for you. Search out the words of Jesus and begin to know your Creator.

Heavenly Father, I want to know You more.
I believe that You are alive and are working in
my heart. I praise Your great name! I cannot
fully comprehend Your love for me or why You
care for me, but I want to seek You. I ask that
You would give me the gift of faith. I don't
understand everything yet, but I want to know
You are always with me. Help my unbelief!
Please open up my heart to hear Your words
of life so that I can follow after You all
the days of my life.

Father God, thank You for loving me and wanting a relationship with me. Thank You for being amazing and doing the impossible. I cannot fathom Your power. I cannot fully express my awe at Your creation. I believe You are everywhere, and I see Your handiwork in all of my surroundings. Help me not to run from You. I don't want to hide anything from You anymore. I want to find peace in Christ. I need You. Help me to choose Your peace. Please guide me in a path that is pleasing to You.

The Lord Gives Wisdom

*If you receive my words and treasure up
my commandments with you, making your
ear attentive to wisdom and inclining your
heart to understanding; yes, if you call out for
insight and raise your voice for understanding,
if you seek it like silver and search for it as for
hidden treasures, then you will understand
the fear of the LORD and find the knowledge
of God. For the LORD gives wisdom;
from his mouth come knowledge
and understanding.*

PROVERBS 2:1–6 ESV

Looking for wisdom? Trying to find answers to life's questions? Or maybe you feel like you've made a multitude of bad decisions and you don't even know what wisdom is anymore?

The Bible tells us that God gives wisdom. And He gives it freely without finding fault (James 1:5–7)! The only requirement is that you trust Him. And believe that God's will is best and that He will lead and guide you in making decisions that align with His purposes. He won't hold your past against you when you come to Him in faith.

Pastor and author C. H. Spurgeon (1834–1892) said this: "We need our God; He is to be had for the seeking; and He will not deny Himself to any one of us if we personally seek His face."

Remember that God is not playing games with you. He has promised in His Word that if you seek Him, you *will* find Him if you seek with all of your heart (Jeremiah 29:13).

While He May Be Found

*Then they will call to me but I will not answer;
they will look for me but will not find me, since they
hated knowledge and did not choose to fear the LORD.
Since they would not accept my advice and spurned
my rebuke. . . . But whoever listens to me will live
in safety and be at ease, without fear of harm.*

PROVERBS 1:28–30, 33 NIV

The great evangelist and founder of Moody Church, D. L. Moody (1837–1899), spoke the following truth over one hundred years ago—it still tugs at heartstrings even today: "No matter how low down you are; no matter what your disposition has been; you may be low in your thoughts, words, and actions; you may be selfish; your heart may be overflowing with corruption and wickedness; yet Jesus will have compassion upon you. He will speak comforting words to you; not treat you coldly or spurn you, as perhaps those of earth would, but will speak tender words, and words of love and affection and kindness. Just come at once. He is a faithful friend—a friend that sticketh closer than a brother."

We can't assume that there will always be time to seek Him. *Later.*

We can't assume that we can live the way we want now until we're ready to settle down and then commit our lives to God. *Later.*

We only have this moment. There is no guarantee of tomorrow. Get serious about God now. Come at once—while He may be found.

As it says in Psalm 32:6 (NLT), "Therefore, let all the godly pray to you while there is still time, that they may not drown in the floodwaters of judgment."

If you're already a believer, commit to pray for your friends and loved ones who don't know God. Ask Him for divine appointments to be able to share His love.

Your Choice

Where can I go from your Spirit? Where can
I flee from your presence? If I go up to the heavens,
you are there; if I make my bed in the depths,
you are there. If I rise on the wings of the dawn,
if I settle on the far side of the sea, even there your
hand will guide me, your right hand will hold me fast.
PSALM 139:7–10 NIV

For some, this scripture passage creates an uncomfortable feeling. You can't hide from God. You can't go through life pretending that God can't see what you're doing in each moment. You know you're headed down a dangerous path, but you're having fun and God can wait.

For others, this scripture creates a sense of peace and calm. You don't have to fear. God is always with you everywhere. Guiding you. Holding you tight. You have trusted Him as your Savior and have faith that He is working all things together for your good and His glory.

Which feeling do you want to take with you? Uncomfortable guilt—or peace?

The peace God gives is beyond our understanding (Philippians 4:6–7). In the middle of grief, trouble, suffering, stress, and the messes we get ourselves in—God offers hope. We can know His peace that comes through a relationship with Him in Christ.

God is everywhere. Colossians 1:17 (NIV) says, "He is before all things, and in him all things hold together." God is holding the universe together in His hands. He is constantly aware of you and constantly with you. Colossians 1 also says that God has reconciled everything "by making peace through his blood, shed on the cross" (v. 20 NIV).

Choose peace.

Everlasting Life

Search me, God, and know my heart; test me and
know my anxious thoughts. See if there is any offensive
way in me, and lead me in the way everlasting.
PSALM 139:23–24 NIV

This section about knowing God has all been leading up to this point: it doesn't matter how much you know *about* God if you don't know Him personally and believe the truth about what He's done for you.

The Bible even says that some who think they know God, really don't (Matthew 7:21–23). You either know God personally—you're living for Him and you've allowed Him to change your life—or you don't. Knowing God personally means you're daily choosing God's will over your own. You're pushing down your own selfish desires and asking God what He would have you do—then doing it!

Jesus said, "I am the way and the truth and the life. No one comes to the Father except through me" (John 14:6 NIV). Be sure. You can't know the Father without coming to faith through His Son.

So what exactly is everlasting life? Jesus answers this Himself: "That they know you, the only true God, and Jesus Christ, whom you have sent" (John 17:3 NIV).

Knowing God through faith in His Son, Jesus Christ, is eternal life itself. Commit your life to Him while He may be found. In this very moment. If you already know Christ as your Savior, pray these verses for your friends and loved ones who haven't come to faith yet.

Heavenly Father, I commit myself to You at this moment and for all eternity. Forgive me for my sins and my selfishness. I believe in Your Son, Jesus Christ, and that You sent Him to save me. I believe there is no other way to everlasting life. I know You're my creator. I know You are holy. There are no words to express my gratitude that You would send Yourself—through Your Son, Jesus—to die on the cross for my sins. So I simply come before You and ask that You would change me. Show me how to live my life knowing You personally.

Lord, I have so many friends and family members that are living their lives just to please themselves. My heart is heavy for them. Please soften their hearts and allow me opportunities to love them. Let my changed life be a testimony to Your love and faithfulness. My actions say a lot more than my words, so let me truly live out a life that makes others want to know You. I don't need to be a Bible-thumper to do that. I don't need to constantly invite them to church to do that. I don't want to turn them off to You, Lord. I just need to live my daily life to please You. Help me to do that.

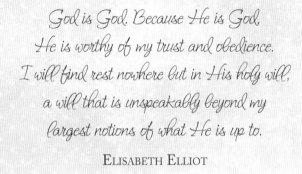

God is God. Because He is God,
He is worthy of my trust and obedience.
I will find rest nowhere but in His holy will,
a will that is unspeakably beyond my
largest notions of what He is up to.

ELISABETH ELLIOT

Trusting God

Unfailing Love

*Answer me quickly, L*ORD*; my spirit fails.*
Do not hide your face from me or I will be like those
who go down to the pit. Let the morning bring me word
of your unfailing love, for I have put my trust in you.
Show me the way I should go, for to you I entrust my life.
*Rescue me from my enemies, L*ORD*, for I hide myself in*
you. Teach me to do your will, for you are my God;
may your good Spirit lead me on level ground.
PSALM 143:7–10 NIV

A woman who had been deeply hurt by life's storms said, "I still love God, but I don't really trust Him any longer. I don't feel protected anymore." But knowing and trusting God go hand in hand.

God's plans and purposes are beyond us. When bad things happen, if you're living in God's will, you can fully trust that God is constantly working everything out for your good and for His glory (Romans 8:28). Make no mistake. God is at work even in your darkest hours.

A major financial crisis can bring about blessings you never thought possible. A death in the family can bring the lost to Christ and bless countless people. A broken marriage can be healed, turning the hardest of hearts into fully committed followers of Christ.

Even when your own poor choices have caused unfortunate circumstances and you feel like there is no hope and no way out—God sees. He is loving and gracious. He welcomes you back into His arms and says, *"I'm here. You are not alone. I will never leave you."*

God's unfailing love is always at work, redeeming you—even if it doesn't feel like it.

Psalm 13:5–6 (NIV) says: "But I trust in your unfailing love; my heart rejoices in your salvation. I will sing the Lord's praise, for he has been good to me."

You can trust in His unfailing love.

In All Your Ways

Trust in the LORD with all your heart and lean not on your own understanding; in all your ways submit to him, and he will make your paths straight.
PROVERBS 3:5–6 NIV

How many times do we set out to do something that was never ours to do? We try to fix a problem that isn't ours to fix. We try to help a situation that we're not meant to help. We often get mixed up in things that don't concern us. Big or small, we often take the reins into our own hands and realize too far in that we should have backed up and sought the Lord's guidance before taking a particular path.

God wants us to acknowledge Him before and during our plans. Does this mean if you've made a poor choice and taken a wrong path that you're on your own? Absolutely not. God has promised to never leave you. Trust Him to help you get back on the path that was meant for you.

Truth is, it might be a little messy trying to disconnect yourself from the situation you've put yourself in! But God is faithful even when we make a mess of things. And once you begin to trust the Lord with all of your heart, you'll begin to seek Him first and trust that He will guide you. You'll remember the messiness of going before God.

In all your ways acknowledge Him *first*, and you'll find yourself on the right path.

Steadfast

But I am like a green olive tree in the house of God.
I trust in the steadfast love of God forever and ever.
I will thank you forever, because you have done it.
I will wait for your name, for it is good,
in the presence of the godly.
PSALM 52:8–9 ESV

The dictionary defines *steadfast* as "unwavering; firmly established" and "firm in purpose." God's love is unwavering. He has firmly established His love for us by sending His Son, Jesus. His purpose for us is clear and firm: love God; love others (Luke 10:27).

The love of God is steadfast. The Bible says we can trust it. Do you?

Take a moment—and a lifetime—and pray that God will help you to trust Him more. While you're at it, pray that God will make you strong, firm, and steadfast in your own faith. Jot down the following verse, and pray it for your friends and family members, too: "And the God of all grace, who called you to his eternal glory in Christ, after you have suffered a little while, will himself restore you and make you strong, firm and steadfast. To him be the power for ever and ever. Amen" (1 Peter 5:10–11 NIV).

Pastor and author Max Lucado says: "God became a man so we could trust him, became a sacrifice so we could know him, and defeated death so we could follow him."

Don't be afraid to follow Him wholeheartedly. His love is steadfast for you. You can trust Him!

Heavenly Father, I'll be honest. Sometimes I have a hard time trusting. I like to take matters into my own hands when I cannot feel Your presence. Forgive me when I rush ahead without You, and please help me to slow down the next time I try to do that! Thank You for Your steadfast love. Please help my own faith to become strong, firm, and steadfast. I pray the same for my family and friends. I want to trust You in all things, big and small. You have always been faithful to me in the past. Help me to remember that truth and never doubt Your goodness.

Dear Jesus, I pray especially for _____ (friend or family member). He/she is struggling to trust You. He/she's been deeply wounded and isn't really sure of Your love and faithfulness anymore. Please be real to him/her. Wrap Your loving arms around him/her and do a healing work. Allow me the opportunity to show love and possibly speak truth into his/her life. Thank You for what You've done in my own life. Give me the confidence to be open, honest, and real as I relate to this person.

Trusted Counselor

*You are my hiding place; you will protect me from
trouble and surround me with songs of deliverance.
I will instruct you and teach you in the way you
should go; I will counsel you with my loving eye on
you. . . . Many are the woes of the wicked, but the
LORD's unfailing love surrounds the one who trusts in
him. Rejoice in the LORD and be glad, you righteous;
sing, all you who are upright in heart!*
PSALM 32:7–8, 10–11 NIV

Be completely honest with yourself for a moment: When you receive bad news, who do you call first? When you're in crisis mode, where do you automatically turn without even thinking? Is it God? Do you get on your knees and ask your Lord and Savior for wisdom and comfort? Or do you turn to friends and family first?

When we are hurting or facing a crisis, we often want human touch and human wisdom. There is nothing wrong with that! In fact, the Lord wants us to comfort one another and bear one another's burdens. But He also wants us to go to Him immediately with all of our needs, worries, and burdens (1 Peter 5:7). Because He cares more than anyone else ever will. He offers the ultimate wisdom and comfort.

What a comfort and relief these verses are to those of us who trust in God! God says: *I will instruct you and teach you! I will show you which way to go. I will counsel you. I will watch over you!* What powerful promises to take hold of! Write them down. Post them where you can remember them every single day.

When you need counsel and comfort, get in the habit of going to your divine Counselor first.

Seek and Trust

But the LORD sits enthroned forever; he has established his throne for justice, and he judges the world with righteousness; he judges the peoples with uprightness. The LORD is a stronghold for the oppressed, a stronghold in times of trouble. And those who know your name put their trust in you, for you, O LORD, have not forsaken those who seek you.
PSALM 9:7–10 ESV

When you have walked with God through life for any amount of time, you experience His absolute faithfulness. This brings trust—a deep knowing—that God is ultimately good and has your best interests in mind.

Things happen along the way that don't make any sense to us at the time. We experience pain and sadness that come with living in a fallen, messed-up world. We begin to relate with the truth of 2 Corinthians 4:8–9 (NLT): "We are pressed on every side by troubles, but we are not crushed. We are perplexed, but not driven to despair. We are hunted down, but never abandoned by God. We get knocked down, but we are not destroyed."

As we seek God, we begin to see purpose in our troubles. That same scripture passage goes on to say, "Through suffering, our bodies continue to share in the death of Jesus so that the life of Jesus may also be seen in our bodies" (v. 10 NLT).

God has purpose in everything. He is just. He is righteous, and He is good.

Clear Insight for Living

*The instructions of the L*ord *are perfect, reviving the soul. The decrees of the L*ord *are trustworthy, making wise the simple. The commandments of the L*ord *are right, bringing joy to the heart. The commands of the L*ord *are clear, giving insight for living.*
Psalm 19:7–8 NLT

Part of trusting God is trusting in the truth of His Word. As believers, we trust that the Bible is the inspired Word of God. Second Timothy 3:16 tells us that all scripture is God-breathed. What an amazing concept! God breathed the words of scripture through chosen believers in centuries past, and He has used it to change the lives of countless people who read it and follow Him.

How can we know the Bible is true? Don't be afraid to search out the truth for yourself. Many atheists have been converted by trying to prove the Bible wrong! AnswersInGenesis.org says this about the Bible: "It has been confirmed countless times by archaeology and other sciences. It possesses divine insight into the nature of the universe and has made correct predictions about distant future events with perfect accuracy."

God's instructions in the Bible are clear, and they give us insight for living even now. The Word of God can be trusted. If you want to know how to live your life for God. . . If you need wisdom for today and hope for tomorrow. . . If you want to hear God speak to you in the twenty-first century. . . Get in God's Word. It will change your life!

My Times Are in Your Hands

But I trust in you, Lord; I say, "You are my God."
My times are in your hands; deliver me from the
hands of my enemies, from those who pursue me.
Psalm 31:14–15 niv

Day-to-day trusting God keeps you from being sucked into the constant chaos of life. Where crisis surrounds and drama abounds. Trusting God makes our problems seem so much smaller in light of eternity. While life may be painful and confusing at times, we know that our times are in God's hands. He sees it all and has a miraculous plan to redeem the chaos.

So when trouble comes knocking at your door—and it will—you don't have to freak out! You can say, "I trust in You, Lord! My times are in Your hands. I know You've got this. I trust Your faithfulness. This looks hard, but I know it'll be okay."

Psalm 31:19 (NIV) says: "How abundant are the good things that you have stored up for those who fear you, that you bestow in the sight of all, on those who take refuge in you."

When you trust God, He becomes your refuge—a very present help in times of trouble (Psalm 46:1). A *very present* help. Ponder that. Be amazed at that. Be thankful for that!

God is very present. His power and comfort are constantly available to you. We live in a broken world—but we have *hope*! Because our times are in His hands. His perfect plan is trustworthy.

Heavenly Father, in the midst of the chaos and messes of my life, I need the peace that only You offer. I'm not asking that You take away all of my problems, because I know that this world has trouble; I'm asking that You would go before me and help me not to worry. Increase my faith in You. Help me to trust You no matter what kind of trouble comes knocking at my door. I know I worry unnecessarily, because You've always been faithful in the past. None of these issues surprises You. Help me to trust You more and to stress less.

Lord, I hide myself in You. You are my rock. You are my refuge! Lead me and guide me. All my times are in Your hands. Thank You for offering hope in the midst of chaos. Peace in the midst of life's drama. I'm so amazed that Your presence is available to me, that the power of Your Spirit lives inside of me to whisper Your truth and comfort to me at all times. What an incredible blessing! Help me to seek You in all things, big and small. Thank You for caring about every aspect of my life.

It's not about you.

RICK WARREN, *THE PURPOSE DRIVEN LIFE*

A Life of Worship

Loving God

Let love and faithfulness never leave you;
bind them around your neck, write them on the
tablet of your heart. Then you will win favor
and a good name in the sight of God and man.
PROVERBS 3:3–4 NIV

To love God, you have to know and understand certain things about Him. John 10:27–30 (NIV) says, "My sheep listen to my voice; I know them, and they follow me. I give them eternal life, and they shall never perish; no one will snatch them out of my hand. My Father, who has given them to me, is greater than all; no one can snatch them out of my Father's hand. I and the Father are one." Jesus tells us that He is one with the Father. And Colossians 1:15–20 tells us that Jesus is the image of the invisible God.

In John 15 Jesus tells us how we can show our love for God: by obeying His commands. What are His commands? To love God and love others. Everything else rests on those two things (Matthew 22:36–40).

In biblical times, a gentle shepherd would love and care for his sheep with compassion and kindness. The sheep would listen to the shepherd's voice. Jesus calls us His sheep. In the same way, Jesus wants us to love Him by learning to listen to His voice. Get to know His voice by reading His word and talking to Him throughout your day.

Love God with all your heart and be faithful to obey His words. This pleases God.

Letting God Love Us

I love you, LORD; you are my strength. The LORD is my rock, my fortress, and my savior; my God is my rock, in whom I find protection. He is my shield, the power that saves me, and my place of safety. I called on the LORD, who is worthy of praise, and he saved me from my enemies.
PSALM 18:1–3 NLT

Maybe you've allowed God to save you—but do you let Him love you? How many of us live our daily lives in the knowledge that God actually *delights* in us? As believers, we seek Him for the forgiveness of our sins and know that He died to save us, but do we really believe that He loves and delights in us?

Sometimes it's hard to let God love us when we haven't been able to forgive ourselves for past mistakes. God tells us in His Word that He forgives our sins and chooses not to remember them (Hebrews 8:12). God has wiped out our most shameful secrets through the death and life of Jesus Christ. He forgives you and loves you like no one else ever can. Starting today, don't give in to the lies of the enemy. Shut him down with truth from God's Word.

Start living your everyday life knowing that God delights in you! Write yourself a blessing using key scriptures, and post it in a prominent place so you'll see it each morning before you leave the house. Make a copy for your car, too. Your blessing can sound something like this:

I am a forgiven and dearly loved
child of God. Jesus lives in my heart,
and no enemy can stand against me.
I will live this day letting my light
shine for all the world to see.

Recognize the Lord

O nations of the world, recognize the LORD; recognize
that the LORD is glorious and strong. Give to the LORD
the glory he deserves! Bring your offering and come into
his courts. Worship the LORD in all his holy splendor.
Let all the earth tremble before him.
PSALM 96:7–9 NLT

Years ago in a prominent national newspaper, the religion editor responded to people wanting more evidence for God. They weren't convinced. They wanted a sign. They wanted God to show up on the White House lawn and claim that He was real.

To look outside at the phenomenal creation we live in or to gaze at any human being and recognize the miraculous intricacies of the human body, and then to demand further proof of the existence of God is almost laughable! God wants us to recognize His hand in every-thing. This is part of worship. Recognizing that God is the creator and sustainer of our world and everything in it. Thanking Him for it and being good stewards of all He has given us.

If you're not in the habit of recognizing God in everything, you can change that. First ask God to help you recognize His hand in all things. Thank Him for your life and the lives of your loved ones. Give thanks for the place you live and the natural beauty of the landscape surrounding you. Look at the night sky, and thank God for knowing you personally in the midst of billions of people. Worship Him for His goodness and His strength.

Keep your eyes open, and recognize the Lord in all things.

Strength and Peace through Worship

*Honor the LORD, you heavenly beings; honor the LORD
for his glory and strength. Honor the LORD for the glory
of his name. Worship the LORD in the splendor of his
holiness. . . . The LORD gives his people strength.
The LORD blesses them with peace.*
PSALM 29:1–2, 11 NLT

When we worship the Lord, He gives us His strength and peace. Second Corinthians 1:21–22 (NIV) says: "Now it is God who makes both us and you stand firm in Christ. He anointed us, set his seal of ownership on us, and put his Spirit in our hearts as a deposit, guaranteeing what is to come." How powerful! God has put His very own Spirit in our hearts—the Holy Spirit. He makes us stand firm in Christ. We are His. We have a guarantee of what is to come!

When our eyes are focused on Christ in worship, we rise above the storms of life. And like Peter, when we get distracted and scared by the waves around us, we start to sink. Peter cried out to God for help when he realized how crazy and unbelievable it was to step out in faith. But the Bible says that "immediately Jesus reached out his hand and caught him" (Matthew 14:31 NIV).

Are you having trouble stepping out in faith? Are you longing for strength and peace? Are you sinking in the storms of life? Ask God to reach out His hand and catch you. Ask Him to forgive you for doubting. Keep your eyes trained on Him, and He will give you strength and peace in all situations.

I love You, O Lord, my strength (Psalm 18:1).
I want to show my love for You by obeying
Your commands. Help me to love others like
You want me to. I worship You and recognize
You for who You are. I'm in awe of all that You
have done. I praise You in the morning for each
new day. I thank You for my family and friends.
My heart is full because of Your salvation.
Thank You for Your love, strength, and peace.
Thank You for the promise of everlasting life!
I will be glad and rejoice in You; I will sing
praise to Your name (Psalm 9:2).

You have forgiven my sins. Help me to forgive myself. Allow me to believe the truth that You delight in me and want to be my friend. Because of what Jesus did for me on the cross, I can come to You with confidence. Lord, that is so amazing to me! Thank You! Help me to step out in faith believing that Your power—the same power that raised Christ from the grave— is available to me on a constant basis. Let me live that I may praise You (Psalm 119:175).

True, Everyday Worship

Exalt the Lord our God and
worship at his footstool; he is holy.
PSALM 99:5 NIV

Worship is more than the weekly service at church on Sundays. Though that is definitely a part of worship, true, everyday worship means so much more. Jesus says in John 4:23–24 (NIV), "Yet a time is coming and has now come when the true worshipers will worship the Father in the Spirit and in truth, for they are the kind of worshipers the Father seeks. God is spirit, and his worshipers must worship in the Spirit and in truth."

Churches are often full of Sunday-only worshippers. Those who pretend to love God on Sundays but disregard Him the rest of the week. They want to be seen at church, but come Monday morning they are back to living for themselves. Jesus says that those people honor Him with their lips, but their hearts are actually far from God (Matthew 15:8).

Are you honoring God with your lips? That's great! But make sure your heart is in it, too. God wants us to live our lives in true, everyday worship. This is a daily laying down of your own selfish desires and following Christ. This is viewing the mundane tasks of life as acts of service to God. (Yep, doing the laundry, scrubbing the bathrooms, and preparing food for your family can actually be acts of worship to God when done in the right spirit!) This is accepting each challenge and blessing with grace and recognizing God's hand in the midst of it all.

Don't be just a Sunday worshipper. Live every day as an act of worship.

My Time

Deal bountifully with your servant, that I may live and keep your word. Open my eyes, that I may behold wondrous things out of your law. I am a sojourner on the earth; hide not your commandments from me! My soul is consumed with longing for your rules at all times.
PSALM 119:17–20 ESV

If only there were a few more hours in the day! How often do we hear people use that phrase? The problem is that if *you're* the one wishing for that, you are busier than God ever intended you to be.

Ephesians 5:15–17 (NIV) says, "Be very careful, then, how you live—not as unwise but as wise, making the most of every opportunity, because the days are evil. Therefore do not be foolish, but understand what the Lord's will is."

Basically, don't waste your time on things you're not supposed to be doing. We may be spending our time doing a lot of really great things: service projects, Sunday school, singing in the church choir, volunteering at soup kitchens, or baking cookies for schools. But one person can't do all of those things, and believe it or not, God doesn't ask that of us. Sometimes we have to let go of really good things in order to make time in our lives for the very best things—God things—the activities and projects that He has for us.

Be consumed with what God wants you to do. Not what your well-meaning Christian friends and family want you to do. Ask God to show you what is most important, and spend your time joyfully serving Him in those areas with all of your heart.

My Gifts and Talents

Like clouds and wind without rain is
a man who boasts of a gift he does not give.
PROVERBS 25:14 ESV

Each of us is gifted with something that God wants to use. Pastor and author Rick Warren says in *The Purpose Driven Life*, "You were made for God, not vice versa, and life is about letting God use you for his purposes, not your using him for your own purposes."

First Peter 4:10–11 (NIV) says, "Each of you should use whatever gift you have received to serve others, as faithful stewards of God's grace in its various forms. If anyone speaks, they should do so as one who speaks the very words of God. If anyone serves, they should do so with the strength God provides, so that in all things God may be praised through Jesus Christ. To him be the glory and the power for ever and ever. Amen."

Our gifts and talents are encouraged through our school-age years, and we grow up honing our skills to be the best that they can be. Though it is good to work at mastering our skills, God wants us to do this for His glory and not for our own agendas.

It is important to remember that for a Christian, God is your promoter. If He wants to use your gifts and abilities in prominent places in this life, He will make that happen. And if that is not in His will for you, no amount of striving or manipulating will get you where you think you want to be. Think of it this way: not every pretty voice is meant to sing on stage. The lullabies a mother sings to her child are just as worshipful and pleasing to the Lord as any soloist singing in front of a church.

The point of this devotion is this: yes, do your very best and work at your skills and abilities to make them excellent—but do it for God's glory, and allow Him to use you according to His plan.

My Treasure

*In the house of the righteous there is much treasure,
but trouble befalls the income of the wicked.*
PROVERBS 15:6 ESV

Christians shut down sometimes when it comes to
money. Some say, "God, You can have Your way with
me, but keep my money out of it!" The truth is that our
heartstrings are often tied up with our purse strings! You
can generally look at a person's bank account and find out
what matters most to him or her.

The Bible says that "where your treasure is, there your heart will be also" (Matthew 6:21 NIV). Are you worshipping God with your money? Not just giving the church a few dollars here or there or contributing to the building fund—but actually laying it all on the line and saying, "God—this is really Yours. You've blessed me with this income, and I will do with it what You would have me do."

There can be a lot of guilt equated with money, too. Don't listen to the lies of the enemy. Ask forgiveness for what you've done with your money in the past if you need to and move on. Start living for God with your money today.

Malachi 3:10 (NIV) says, " 'Bring the whole tithe into the storehouse, that there may be food in my house. Test me in this,' says the LORD Almighty, 'and see if I will not throw open the floodgates of heaven and pour out so much blessing that there will not be room enough to store it.' "

Seek the Lord on this one, and don't be afraid to do what He is calling you to do. He will bless you for it. Test Him and see!

Heavenly Father, I am praying to You because I know You will answer, O God. Bend down and listen as I pray. Show me Your unfailing love in wonderful ways. By Your mighty power You rescue those who seek refuge from their enemies. Guard me as You would guard Your own eyes. Hide me in the shadow of Your wings (Psalm 17). I praise and worship You for protecting me. You always comfort me. Thank You for Your great love. Show me what it means to be an everyday worshipper. I want to worship in the Spirit and in truth.

Lord, I thank You for the gifts and talents You have given me. I pray that You would help me to strive for excellence in my skills, but that I would do so in Your honor. Forgive me for the times I let my ego get in the way. Give me an eternal perspective. All of this is about You and for You. I thank You for this day and the time You've given me. Help me use it wisely. And thank You for the financial blessings You have given me. Help me to give back in a way that pleases You.

It is never God's will that we should be anything less than absolutely complete in Him. Anything that disturbs rest in Him must be cured at once, and it is not cured by being ignored, but by coming to Jesus Christ. If we come to Him and ask Him to produce Christ-consciousness, He will always do it until we learn to abide in Him.

OSWALD CHAMBERS, *My Utmost for His Highest*

Moment by
Moment with God

Abiding

*Show me your ways, L*ORD*, teach me your paths.*
Guide me in your truth and teach me, for you are
God my Savior, and my hope is in you all day long.
PSALM 25:4–5 NIV

Does it astound you that the God of the universe wants to have a moment-by-moment relationship with you? He wants to lead you and guide you. He wants your hope to be in Him alone—all day long!

In John 15:4–5 (ESV) Jesus says: "Abide in me, and I in you. As the branch cannot bear fruit by itself, unless it abides in the vine, neither can you, unless you abide in me. I am the vine; you are the branches. Whoever abides in me and I in him, he it is that bears much fruit, for apart from me you can do nothing."

To abide in Christ is more than just putting Him at the top of your priority list. While that is well and good, God wants so much more for each of us. He doesn't want to just be at the top of a list; He wants to be the center of everything that happens in your life: every relationship you are in, every conversation you have, everything you do.

Just as a branch can't bear fruit unless it remains in the vine, neither can we bear fruit for God if we don't remain (abide) in Christ. Invite the Lord to be the center of your life and begin a moment-by-moment relationship with Him.

Guiding Me

Send me your light and your faithful care,
let them lead me; let them bring me to your
holy mountain, to the place where you dwell.
PSALM 43:3 NIV

Moment by moment God is with you and available to guide you through any and every situation. He wants to rejoice with you during times of blessing, He wants to comfort you during times of pain and sadness, and He wants to guide you through times of confusion and decision making Psalm 73:24 (NIV) teaches: "You guide me with your counsel, and afterward you will take me into glory." Jesus promised that the Holy Spirit would come and guide us in all truth (John 16:13). God will guide us as we listen to His Spirit for wisdom during this life, and then He'll take us to heaven.

When we give our lives to Christ, the Holy Spirit miraculously inhabits our souls and we are no longer alone. We don't have to figure things out by ourselves. We don't have to stress like those who have no purpose in life.

John 14:26 (NIV) tells us, "But the Advocate, the Holy Spirit, whom the Father will send in my name, will teach you all things and will remind you of everything I have said to you." Not only is the Spirit alive and working in us at all times, He is constantly reminding us of God's Word.

If you're looking for guidance, get into God's Word and begin listening to the Holy Spirit.

Understanding for Each Moment

Your word is a lamp for my feet, a light on my path. . . . The unfolding of your words gives light; it gives understanding to the simple.
PSALM 119:105, 130 NIV

God's Word is a lamp for our feet. Reading and knowing God's Word provides us with light so our feet know the next steps to take. We are to obey God step-by-step and moment-by-moment. Even when we don't understand what He's doing. Even when obedience doesn't make any sense. If God shared all of the details with us up front, we would most likely run the other way. Instead, He gives us a light for our paths with just enough understanding for the moment.

Imagine that you are hiking in a forest. As darkness approaches, you realize you'd better start setting up camp. You hike a bit farther to find a spot that offers protection from the elements. It's getting darker and darker. You haven't found a safe place yet, so you keep going down the path, your flashlight guiding you so that you can see just enough to stay on the path. You finally find a safe spot and rest easy for the night. In the morning, you look back and realize the path you were on was extremely dangerous. Any wandering to the left or right would have placed you in peril. But you trusted your flashlight, and it provided enough light to get you to safety. If you had seen the condition of the path in the light of day, you would have been too scared to move on toward safety. You would have run the other direction, and that would not have gotten you to where you needed to be.

In the same way, God lights up our paths just enough so that we can see how to obey Him—step-by-step and moment-by-moment.

Heavenly Father, I want to abide in You. Come and be the center of my life. I invite You to be a part of every conversation, every relationship, every moment of my life. Let Your light and Your truth guide me. Thank You for the Holy Spirit who reminds me of Your words and Your will. Give me the desire to get into Your Word and relate to You on a moment-by-moment basis. Help me to discern Your whispers over the noise of life.

Dear Jesus, when I am afraid, I will put my trust in You. When I don't understand, I will put my trust in You. When I just don't feel like it, I will put my trust in You. Let these words be true in my life, not just lip service but a total heart transformation. I want to worship You and live for You in every moment. I ask for Your protection and favor as I follow after You. Be near me, Lord Jesus. Help me to remember Your promise that You will never leave me.

Protection and Favor

But let all who take refuge in you be glad; let them ever sing for joy. Spread your protection over them, that those who love your name may rejoice in you. Surely, LORD, you bless the righteous; you surround them with your favor as with a shield.

PSALM 5:11–12 NIV

The prayer of Jabez in 1 Chronicles 4:10 (NIV) sounds a bit like this prayer of David in the Psalms. Jabez prays: "'Oh, that you would bless me and enlarge my territory! Let your hand be with me, and keep me from harm so that I will be free from pain.' And God granted his request."

Can anyone pray these prayers? Yes! God loves it when we come to Him in prayer with all of our needs, thanks, and desires. But remember that there is no magical prayer to make God do your bidding. When we come to Him in prayer and begin relating to Him on a daily basis, He begins to align our desires with His perfect plan.

Pastor Kirt Henman said that a lot of times people blame God for the bad things that happen to them when really it is their own fault. Absolutely pray for God's protection and favor for you and your family, but also pray that God will keep you from making wrong choices that end in the natural consequences of sin.

If you want God's favor and protection, seek after Him with all your heart and obey Him on a moment-by-moment basis.

Be Near God

But as for me, it is good to be near God.
I have made the Sovereign LORD my refuge;
I will tell of all your deeds.
PSALM 73:28 NIV

Years ago, a youth pastor told his audience to "get so close to God that you smell like Him!" You may wonder how that is even possible. How can an invisible God be close to us?

There is a true story of a premature baby who defied the odds. The parents were told that the baby would not live, and they were not even able to touch her for two months as she was hooked to machines. But God answered the prayers of this family, and she grew into a healthy little girl. At the age of five, the little girl told her mom she smelled God outside. Her mom, knowing that it was an approaching thunderstorm, told her it was just the smell of rain. But the little girl was adamant that it was the smell of God. She told her mom that it smelled like God when you lay your head on His chest.

The Bible says in James 4:8 (NIV) to "come near to God and he will come near to you." And Psalm 145:18 (NIV) tells us that "the LORD is near to all who call on him, to all who call on him in truth."

Just like God was close to the premature baby, He is not far from any of us (Acts 17:27). Even though we can't see the wind, we can feel it and see its effects. But sometimes our "grown-up" faith prevents us from feeling God's presence even though He is always near.

Get back to the faith of a child and get close to God.

Constant Thanks and Never-Ending Praise

May his name endure forever; may it continue as long as the sun. Then all nations will be blessed through him, and they will call him blessed. Praise be to the LORD God, the God of Israel, who alone does marvelous deeds. Praise be to his glorious name forever; may the whole earth be filled with his glory. Amen and Amen.

PSALM 72:17–19 NIV

The Lord delights in prayers like this one. A prayer of constant thanks and never-ending praise, no matter what. In good times and bad. In the midst of devastating loss, Job said, "The LORD gave, and the LORD has taken away; blessed be the name of the LORD" (Job 1:21 ESV).

And Paul tells us, "I know how to live on almost nothing or with everything. I have learned the secret of living in every situation, whether it is with a full stomach or empty, with plenty or little. For I can do everything through Christ, who gives me strength" (Philippians 4:12–13 NLT).

A meaningful and real relationship with God will bring about an eternal perspective in all things. It is a deep faith in Christ that no matter what happens, God is at work. He is trustworthy. He is giving you strength. You can be content no matter the circumstances. You can give praise in every situation.

Author and speaker Louie Giglio says, "God's plans for your life far exceed the circumstances of your day." So give thanks constantly and praise Him in never-ending devotion. His plans are good.

Walking with God

For you have rescued me from death; you have kept my feet from slipping. So now I can walk in your presence, O God, in your life-giving light.
Psalm 56:13 NLT

This moment-by-moment relationship with God we have been discussing, when lived out purposefully, gives us an eternal perspective. Walking with God is not just reading a Bible verse each morning and checking God off your list for the day. It is not being a regular member at church, serving in any capacity that is needed, and leaving faith in the box until the next Sunday.

It is a daily walk with God. It is a continual conversation with, and awareness of, Christ.

"Rejoice always, pray continually, give thanks in all circumstances; for this is God's will for you in Christ Jesus" (1 Thessalonians 5:16–18 NIV).

Walking with God is having a relationship with your Creator. It is knowing Him, loving Him, trusting Him, and worshipping Him in each moment. The Bible promises that we can walk in His presence! In His life-giving light!

Author and twentieth-century preacher Oswald Chambers said, "Ministering as opportunity surrounds us does not mean selecting our surroundings, it means being very selectly God's in any haphazard surroundings which He engineers for us."

We don't get to pick where God uses us. As we walk with God, He wants us to be His in every situation we're faced with. Be "very selectly God's" in every moment.

We praise you, God, we praise you, for your Name is near; people tell of your wonderful deeds" (Psalm 75:1 NIV). Help me to do Your will. To rejoice always, pray continually, give thanks in all circumstances. Give me the ability to praise Your name in everything that comes my way. Show me how to be content. Forgive me for the times I can't see outside of myself. Forgive me for wanting my own way and thinking that I know what is best for me. You are my creator, and Your plans are perfect. Please give me an eternal perspective.

Father God, I pray that You will keep me from making wrong choices that end in the natural consequences of sin. Forgive me for seeking my own agenda at times. Forgive me for wasting time on things that don't really matter. Show me how to walk in Your ways. Please keep my motives pure and my heart set on You. I ask for Your protection and favor as I step out in faith and seek You. Be near me, and help me to trust You with the faith of a child.

There is always the danger that we may just do the work for the sake of the work. This is where the respect and the love and the devotion come in—that we do it to God, to Christ, and that's why we try to do it as beautifully as possible.

MOTHER TERESA

Work That Matters

Working for God

Unless the LORD builds a house, the work of the builders is wasted. Unless the LORD protects a city, guarding it with sentries will do no good.
PSALM 127:1 NLT

Any work you do can be an act of worship if done in the right spirit. Whether you work a nine-to-five job to pay the bills, work in the medical field saving and caring for human life, teach children at a school, or care for young children at home all day, it all has value in the sight of God. One job is not better than another if it is done unto the Lord. And unless God is in it, the Bible says it is wasted!

Your job should not be your sole purpose in life. Furthering your career is nothing if it is not furthering the kingdom. The Bible has a lot to say about our work. Here are just a few important scriptures:

> *Work willingly at whatever you do,*
> *as though you were working for the*
> *Lord rather than for people. Remember*
> *that the Lord will give you an inheritance*
> *as your reward, and that the Master*
> *you are serving is Christ.*
> COLOSSIANS 3:23–24 NLT

> *Work with enthusiasm,*
> *as though you were working for*
> *the Lord rather than for people.*
> EPHESIANS 6:7 NLT

> *Use your hands for good hard work, and*
> *then give generously to others in need.*
> EPHESIANS 4:28 NLT

Since most of us spend all of our days working at something, it's important to seek God in this area. Pray that He would give you wisdom as you seek out His will concerning your work.

Work Hard

A hard worker has plenty of food, but a person who chases fantasies has no sense. . . . Work hard and become a leader; be lazy and become a slave. . . . Lazy people don't even cook the game they catch, but the diligent make use of everything they find.
PROVERBS 12:11, 24, 27 NLT

Good hard work has always been valued. Laziness is never respected. Theologians, inventors, philosophers, and great teachers through the ages talk much about working hard at things that matter.

Thomas Edison said, "Genius is 1 percent inspiration and 99 percent perspiration. Accordingly a genius is often merely a talented person who has done all of his or her homework." He also said, "Opportunity is missed by most people because it is dressed in overalls and looks like work."

Lazy people shouldn't expect others to care for them. We're not talking about taking a rest or a much-needed break after you have worked hard; there is great value in resting! God Himself rested from hard work and wants us to do the same (Genesis 2). We're talking about those who never work hard at anything (not because they are unable, but because they are unwilling) and still expect to be fed and cared for. That is a completely unbiblical view. The Bible even says if you don't work, you don't eat (2 Thessalonians 3:10)!

Hard work can seem daunting at times, but it is accomplished by taking it one step at a time.

St. Francis of Assisi said, "Start by doing what's necessary, then what's possible; and suddenly you are doing the impossible."

Whatever you decide to do, work at it with all your heart. Don't cut corners. Don't be lazy. Work hard and your needs will be met.

Be Diligent

*A sluggard's appetite is never filled,
but the desires of the diligent are fully satisfied.*
PROVERBS 13:4 NIV

Diligence is defined as "constant and earnest effort to accomplish what is undertaken." Do you have something on your plate right now that you know God is calling you to do? Would you say you are earnest in your effort to accomplish it? Maybe it's something you enjoy doing or maybe it's something you don't. Either way, work done in diligence is work that will be rewarded.

According to author John Maxwell, "Success depends not merely on how well you do the things you enjoy, but how conscientiously you perform those duties you don't." Be diligent in all things. Those you enjoy, and those you don't. The spirit and attitude in which you do the work that you don't enjoy says a lot more about you than how you carry out the work that you do enjoy!

"But one thing I do: Forgetting what is behind and straining toward what is ahead, I press on toward the goal to win the prize for which God has called me heavenward in Christ Jesus. All of us, then, who are mature should take such a view of things. And if on some point you think differently, that too God will make clear to you" (Philippians 3:13–15 NIV).

Forget past mistakes, learn from them, and press on toward the goal. As this verse in Philippians 3 says, if you think differently—if you're not quite there yet, you're not sure you understand that just yet—God will make it clear to you. Ask God to give you an eternal perspective in your work and He will make it clear.

Get Rich Quick

Wealth from get-rich-quick schemes quickly disappears;
wealth from hard work grows over time.
PROVERBS 13:11 NLT

Countless people are looking for ways to "get rich quick."
They think that earning millions quickly and then
relaxing on a yacht in the sunshine is what life is all about.
The Bible teaches differently.

Running after earthly wealth and "things" is a waste
of time because you can't take them with you! John
Ortberg, in his book *When the Game Is Over, It All Goes
Back in the Box*, says that "possessions, my resume, my
body, my money, pleasures, other people's opinions of me,
security, titles and positions, youth, power, physical

attractiveness, and health" all go back in the box at the end of life. These are what you can take with you: "God, other people, [your] soul, and deeds of love."

If your goal in life is to get rich and retire early, you are missing it! Consider this:

> *Keep falsehood and lies far from me; give*
> *me neither poverty nor riches, but give me*
> *only my daily bread. Otherwise, I may have*
> *too much and disown you and say, "Who is*
> *the LORD?" Or I may become poor and steal,*
> *and so dishonor the name of my God.*
> PROVERBS 30:8–9 NIV

The writer of this proverb is asking that God not give him poverty, but he is also asking that God not give him riches! Can you believe that? He knows that the heart of man sometimes forgets the Lord when he has no need of Him.

Are you striving to get rich quick on earth? Why not strive instead to be rich in Christ and eternal relationships? That is what will last forever.

Heavenly Father, Please help me work willingly at whatever I do, and help me remember that it is all about You and for You anyway! Help me to think eternally, and let that show in my work. Keep me from laziness and greed. Help me to work hard at the tasks You've given me and to do the ones I don't enjoy with a good attitude. Thank You for giving me the ability to work and the skills I need to do a good job. I ask that You would bless my work and that I'd be able to bless others by the income I earn from it.

Lord, I've made a lot of mistakes in this life. And mistakes concerning my attitude toward work and my career. I keep beating myself up over it. Please allow me to forget my past mistakes and press on toward the goal: YOU! I want to learn from my failures so that I don't repeat them, but I also don't want to keep repeating them in my mind. Thank You for Your forgiveness and grace. Help me to forgive myself and to keep my focus on Your will for me. Allow me to work with purpose and be rich in You!

Just Do It!

*If you plan to do evil, you will be lost; if you plan
to do good, you will receive unfailing love and
faithfulness. Work brings profit, but mere talk
leads to poverty! Wealth is a crown for the wise;
the effort of fools yields only foolishness.*
PROVERBS 14:22–24 NLT

Organizations, schools, businesses, and churches have
meetings. Lots of meetings. This committee gets together
to do this thing, and that committee gets together to do
that thing. A good leader knows when it's important to
have a meeting and when it's important to get to work. A
good leader casts a vision for the group and sees results.
A poor leader will let a pointless meeting continue until
everyone gets to hear themselves talk. Poor leaders are
ineffective and waste their time and everyone else's
time, too.

The Bible says that mere talk leads to poverty. You have to actually do the work you've talked about doing. Stop talking and start working!

Thomas Jefferson said: "Determine never to be idle. No person will have occasion to complain of the want of time who never loses any. It is wonderful how much may be done if we are always doing."

This is tough stuff for those of us with mountains of to-do lists and tasks that we've been putting off for months, or even years! Those jobs that have to be done, but nobody wants to do them? Ask God to give you the energy to tackle them one at a time. Be a good leader of yourself—and whatever teams you may be on. Stop talking about the fact that you have been putting it off— and just do it. Think how happy you'll feel to have the task behind you. Just do it!

Prosperity, Hard Work,
and Workaholism

Good planning and hard work lead to prosperity,
but hasty shortcuts lead to poverty. Wealth created by
a lying tongue is a vanishing mist and a deadly trap.
PROVERBS 21:5–6 NLT

Do you want to prosper? Who *doesn't* want to prosper? The Bible gives us a formula for prosperity. If you have integrity, you plan well, and you work hard—scripture tells us that leads to prosperity! Again, this is not a get-rich-quick gospel! Prosperity takes hard work.

We've all heard it said that it's important to work smarter and *not* harder. Proverbs supports that phrase. *Good planning* and *hard work* lead to prosperity. You have to plan smart before you work hard. This will help to keep you from working *too* hard.

Working too hard and becoming a workaholic is just as dangerous as being lazy. Politician John Capozzi wrote, "The executive who works from 7:00 a.m. to 7:00 p.m. every day will be both very successful and fondly remembered by his wife's next husband."

"It is useless for you to work so hard from early morning until late at night, anxiously working for food to eat; for God gives rest to his loved ones" (Psalm 127:2 NLT).

It's so important to balance hard-work ethics with eternal perspectives. The Bible says that God gives rest to those He loves, so stop working *too* hard. Those of you with workaholic tendencies, pray for God to give you balance in these areas.

Ruined

Despite their desires, the lazy will come to ruin,
for their hands refuse to work. Some people are
always greedy for more, but the godly love to give!
PROVERBS 21:25–26 NLT

God's Word has a lot to say about greed. It is even listed along with some major sins! Now we know that a sin is a sin. But some sins have worse consequences. The Bible says that greed has some pretty awful results! Check them out:

The greedy bring ruin to their households,
but the one who hates bribes will live.
PROVERBS 15:27 NIV

The greedy stir up conflict, but those who
trust in the LORD will prosper.
PROVERBS 28:25 NIV

I was enraged by their sinful
greed; I punished them, and hid
my face in anger, yet they kept
on in their willful ways.
ISAIAH 57:17 NIV

Woe to you, teachers of the law and Pharisees, you hypocrites! You clean the outside of the cup and dish, but inside they are full of greed and self-indulgence.
MATTHEW 23:25 NIV

Then he said to them, "Watch out! Be on your guard against all kinds of greed; life does not consist in an abundance of possessions."
LUKE 12:15 NIV

For of this you can be sure: No immoral, impure or greedy person—such a person is an idolater—has any inheritance in the kingdom of Christ and of God.
EPHESIANS 5:5 NIV

Do you not know that wrongdoers will not inherit the kingdom of God? Do not be deceived: Neither the sexually immoral nor idolaters nor adulterers nor men who have sex with men nor thieves nor the greedy nor drunkards nor slanderers nor swindlers will inherit the kingdom of God.
1 CORINTHIANS 6:9–10 NIV

Steer clear of greed to avoid ruin!

A Good Example

She gets up while it is still night; she provides food for her family and portions for her female servants. She considers a field and buys it; out of her earnings she plants a vineyard. She sets about her work vigorously; her arms are strong for her tasks. She sees that her trading is profitable, and her lamp does not go out at night. . . . She opens her arms to the poor and extends her hands to the needy. When it snows, she has no fear for her household; for all of them are clothed in scarlet.

PROVERBS 31:15–18, 20–21 NIV

Abraham Lincoln said, "Whatever you are, be a good one." Whatever job you've chosen to pursue—whether it's a professional career, owning your own business, or managing your household as a wife and mom—do it with all your soul.

The Proverbs 31 woman was the original work-from-home mom. She ran a successful business and took care of her family while seeking to honor the Lord in everything. She is an example for us all. Although following in her footsteps may seem daunting, pray that God will instill the same work ethic and ability inside of you.

Remember what Mother Teresa advised: "Give the world the best you have, and it may never be enough; give the world the best you've got anyway. You see, in the final analysis, it is between you and God; it was never between you and them anyway."

That is why your work is so important. It's between you and God. So give Him your very best. That's all that really matters.

Lord, I pray for balance in my work life. Help me to work hard but not so hard that I neglect You and my friends and family. I've been putting off things that need to get done. Please give me energy and the desire to do what needs to happen with a right spirit. Thank You for the wonderful examples You've shown me of people who honor You with their work. Help me be more like the Proverbs 31 woman who honors You and whose husband and children respect her for her hard work and attitude.

Greed is a scary thing that creeps up on me unawares. Search out any greed You see in me and pluck it out, Lord, I beg You! Help me to give more and want less. I praise You and thank You for 1 Corinthians 6:11 (NIV), which says, "And that is what some of you *were*. But you were washed, you were sanctified, you were justified in the name of the Lord Jesus Christ and by the Spirit of our God" (emphasis added). Thank You, Father, for washing me clean. Thank You for Jesus and Your Spirit working inside me to make me more like You.

Attitude, to me, is more important than facts. It is more important than the past, than education, than money, than circumstances, than failures, than successes, than what other people think or say or do. It is more important than appearance, giftedness, or skill. It will make or break a company. . .a church. . .a home.

CHARLES R. SWINDOLL

Family Matters

A Good Attitude

Do not harden your hearts, as at Meribah, as on the day at Massah in the wilderness, when your fathers put me to the test and put me to the proof, though they had seen my work. For forty years I loathed that generation and said, "They are a people who go astray in their heart, and they have not known my ways." Therefore I swore in my wrath, "They shall not enter my rest."
PSALM 95:8–11 ESV

Why is having a good attitude in the section on family matters? Your attitude truly makes all the difference when it comes to family and family issues. You can have a fully dysfunctional *Everybody Loves Raymond* kind of family and still head to family functions without dread in your heart if you have a good attitude.

It has been said that every family is dysfunctional if it is made up of more than one person. So don't feel sorry for yourself; instead, start cultivating a good attitude. Every family has its issues. Every family has problems that they don't want the whole world knowing. But *every family* has them. You are not alone in thinking that your extended family is the craziest or the worst. Take a little comfort in knowing that lots of people feel that way— about their own family, that is. Not yours!

But you have a choice: you can either hightail it outta there as soon as you are old enough and never go home again, or you can change your attitude and learn how to love the maybe-not-so-lovable. It's an attitude thing. Let's dig into God's Word in this section and find out what He wants us to know about family matters.

Forgiveness

Do not hold against us the sins of past generations;
may your mercy come quickly to meet us, for we
are in desperate need. Help us, God our Savior,
for the glory of your name; deliver us and forgive
our sins for your name's sake.
PSALM 79:8–9 NIV

Nineteenth-century poet, writer, and playwright Oscar Wilde said, "After a good dinner one can forgive anybody, even one's own relatives." Family and forgiveness go hand in hand. Families are made up of a bunch of imperfect people—some trying to follow the Lord and some very far from God. But God calls us to love them all—and to forgive.

Max Lucado said, "Forgiveness is unlocking the door to set someone free and realizing you were the prisoner!" Forgiveness is not about sweeping things under the rug and pretending. Forgiveness is bold. It is facing the facts about people and their sinful natures, and choosing to love and forgive in spite of hurt and hard feelings.

Bitterness will choke you. Ignorance is *not* bliss. But forgiveness will set you free.

The Bible tells us plainly that if we want God to forgive us, we have to be willing to forgive others (Matthew 6:14). Forgiveness and love do not mean that you let people walk all over you. Or that you stay in an abusive relationship. It just means that you go before God, share your hurts and feelings about your family with Him, and ask Him to help you love and forgive them *His* way.

Don't be a prisoner because you're refusing to forgive. Let go and allow God to change your heart and set you free.

Loving the Unlovely

Hatred stirs up quarrels,
but love makes up for all offenses.
PROVERBS 10:12 NLT

You may have a lot of hurt in your family. The relatives in your life may have caused you more harm than good during your lifetime. This is true for many people. Even so, God calls us to love the unlovely. Jesus says in Luke 6:32 (NIV), "If you love those who love you, what credit is that to you? Even sinners love those who love them." Of course you love the people who genuinely love you back. Jesus says even sinners do that! But God wants us to go much further and actually love our enemies. And sadly, sometimes our own family members have become our enemies.

"Above all, love each other deeply, because love covers over a multitude of sins" (1 Peter 4:8 NIV). So the question becomes, how do you love those that you can't even stand to be around?

First, you pray for God to change your heart and give you His love for that family member. Through that heart change, you'll be able to forgive them and get God's perspective on the situation. There are always three sides to every issue: your side, the other person's side, and God's view (what *really* happened!).

It's not easy to put yourself in someone else's shoes. And the Bible warns us to be careful when we judge someone (Matthew 7:1–2). When you judge someone without understanding their situation, you'll often be put in a very similar situation during your lifetime ("the measure you use will be used on you"). God allows things like that to happen so you can understand and forgive those you harbor bitter feelings toward.

Pray for God to help you not to judge others and to forgive the unlovable in your life.

The Family Gossip

The mouths of fools are their undoing, and their lips
are a snare to their very lives. The words of a gossip
are like choice morsels; they go down to the inmost parts.
PROVERBS 18:7–8 NIV

Families often make light of gossip and even encourage it under the guise of "just wanting to help." But we all know that gossip hurts. No one likes to walk into a room only to hear "the hush" and realize they were the topic of discussion. Sadly, this often happens during special occasions and holidays. And the truth is, it is easy to participate in the family gossip. It can sneak up on you when you are least expecting it. Aunt Martha innocently asks how your out-of-town brother is doing, and soon she's telling you that she heard something awful about him that you should be praying about!

Leo Aikman said this: "You can tell more about a person by what he says about others than you can by what others say about him." If Aunt Martha is going to say bad things about your brother, she is likely to say bad things about you, too. And if you're always worried about what other people are saying about you behind your back, maybe *you* are saying a little too much about everyone else! Don't let your mouth be your undoing. Ask the Lord to help you keep a tight rein on your tongue (James 1:26).

Don't participate in the family gossip. It doesn't help anyone!

Heavenly Father, I pray that You will change my attitude toward my family. Sometimes I don't feel like loving them, and I just want to avoid any family situations that come my way. I'm bitter about some things, and I ask that You would forgive me for that. I have judged them without knowing all the details. I don't want to be in bondage because of bitterness in my heart. Give me Your love for my family, and please give me wisdom as I relate with them. It's a touchy, tedious process that I cannot approach without Your strength.

Dear Jesus, I feel very ashamed for my part in the family gossip. I admit that I easily participate when the conversation gets around to me—and sometimes I do it eagerly! There are days when I just can't wait to share what I've heard about someone else. I know now that this does not honor You, and it only hinders my relationship with my family—and ultimately with You. I'm sorry. Please help me place a tight rein on my tongue. It gets me in so much trouble. Forgive me, and show me how to use my words wisely.

Relationships That Honor God

*Do not envy the wicked, do not desire their company;
for their hearts plot violence, and their lips talk about
making trouble. By wisdom a house is built, and through
understanding it is established; through knowledge its
rooms are filled with rare and beautiful treasures.*
PROVERBS 24:1–4 NIV

This proverb begins by explaining the trouble we can get in when we are in relationships that don't honor God—with people who don't honor God. But the Bible says that by wisdom a house is built, a home is built, relationships are built. God wants us to seek His wisdom as we relate to our family members.

This proverb can be taken literally: wise people can have the knowledge and understanding to build a house with their own hands and the industriousness to work hard and fill it with beautiful treasures. It can also mean that we build our homes and families with wisdom and understanding that come from God. Our "treasures" don't necessarily need to have monetary value. They can be family values such as love, respect, and charity.

When we work hard at trying to be more understanding in our relationships, we become less selfish. We listen more and talk less. We ask for less and give more. When we honor God in our relationships, His will comes first. We seek to please Him as we relate to one another. Ask God to be the center of all of your relationships so that they will honor Him.

For Wives: Part 1

A wife of noble character who can find? She is worth far more than rubies. Her husband has full confidence in her and lacks nothing of value. She brings him good, not harm, all the days of her life.
PROVERBS 31:10–12 NIV

A wife who honors God will bring her husband good and not harm, all the days of her life. Is that your goal as a wife? Ephesians 5:33 (NIV) says, "Each one of you also must love his wife as he loves himself, and the wife must respect her husband."

Emerson Eggerichs wrote a book based on this verse called *Love and Respect*. The whole truth of the matter is that if our husbands feel that we are respecting them, they will love us. Without respect, the husband reacts without love, causing the wife to react without respect. Eggerichs calls it "the crazy cycle."

It can be extremely difficult to treat your husband with respect right after he has said or done something that felt unloving, but someone has to stop the crazy cycle, or it just continues. It's like the song that never ends.

As women, we don't think much about it sometimes, but disrespect cuts a man to the core. That's why the Bible says a man needs respect. A woman needs love. You can't have one without the other. And a marriage won't work without both.

Respecting your husband by the way you talk to him and treat him in public, in private, and especially in front of the kids will bring him good and not harm, all the days of his life.

For Wives: Part 2

*Better to live on a corner of the roof
than share a house with a quarrelsome wife.*
PROVERBS 21:9 NIV

Apparently this verse is worth repeating because Proverbs
25:24 says the exact same thing. The New Living Trans-
lation says it a little more humorously: "It's better to live
alone in the corner of an attic than with a quarrelsome
wife in a lovely home."

And Proverbs 27:15–16 (NLT) says: "A quarrelsome wife is as annoying as constant dripping on a rainy day. Stopping her complaints is like trying to stop the wind or trying to hold something with greased hands."

While we may chuckle at these scriptures a bit, it's so important to see the truth in this wisdom. A woman who argues with her husband all the time has forgotten how to be his friend.

When couples have been married for a while, it's so easy to slip into a comfortable-ness where we take our husbands' love for granted. We disregard their feelings sometimes thinking that they'll love us no matter what. We forget that they need our respect, and we begin to talk to them like one of the children.

Take a step back and think about your relationship for a moment. If you're not feeling loved and cherished, is it because you have stopped respecting your husband? Sometimes we say things to our husbands that we would never say to our friends.

Remember to treat your husband like you would a friend (just like you did when he was first attracted to you!), and he'll become one again. If that seems impossible—that your marriage has gone too far in the opposite direction—remember that God is the God of the impossible!

It's not too late to start over.

For Moms

She is clothed with strength and dignity; she can laugh at the days to come. She speaks with wisdom, and faithful instruction is on her tongue. She watches over the affairs of her household and does not eat the bread of idleness. Her children arise and call her blessed; her husband also, and he praises her: "Many women do noble things, but you surpass them all."

PROVERBS 31:25–29 NIV

Wouldn't it be fabulous if your children would arise and call you blessed every morning? Most days a mom has to stir cranky kids out of bed (sometimes with great effort and force!), try to get them to eat something that resembles a healthy breakfast, rush them through the brushing of their teeth and changing into (hopefully) clean clothes before the bus comes. The kids usually forget the "calling Mom blessed" part.

Being a mom is a noble (and difficult, and stressful, and exciting, and emotional, and exhausting, and priceless, and wonderful) calling. Hannah Whitall Smith said, "The mother is and must be—whether she knows it or not—the greatest, strongest, and most lasting teacher her children have." Whew! That's a lot of pressure! But that's just the thing: we cannot do it alone—and we're not expected to. We need the power of Christ to strengthen us to do this colossal job, and He is with us during every moment.

Remember, moms: you are never alone! God is with you and available to you at all times and during every situation you find yourself in with your children. Your children are ultimately in God's hands. Worry less. Pray more!

Dear Lord, please help me to build my home with wisdom. Forgive me when I envy others instead of being thankful for my own family and the life You have abundantly blessed me with. Help me to be more understanding and loving in my family relationships. Help me to listen more and talk less. Help me to give more without worrying about getting anything in return. Family life can be messy. Help me to relax more around my family and trust that You are in charge.

Heavenly Father, thank You for my husband and children (or my future husband and children!). Help me to be a wife and mom who honors You and the kind of woman that my husband and children are happy to wake up to each day. Sometimes I get stressed about the monumental task of raising children, but I'm so thankful You are here with me during each moment and decision-making process. Thank You for Your love for me and my family. Thank You for caring what happens in my family life.

I am encouraged when I know people care about me not because of what I do, not because of who I am, not because of where I live. Just because they care about me.

DR. DAVID JEREMIAH,
THE POWER OF ENCOURAGEMENT

Wisdom for
Friendships

Friendships That Honor God

One who has unreliable friends soon comes to ruin,
but there is a friend who sticks closer than a brother.
PROVERBS 18:24 NIV

The book of Proverbs has much to say about friendships. Particularly about being wise in the friends you choose. The late Christian author and speaker Zig Ziglar said, "Life is too short to spend your precious time trying to convince a person who wants to live in gloom and doom otherwise. Give lifting that person your best shot, but don't hang around long enough for his or her bad attitude to pull you down. Instead, surround yourself with optimistic people." Does this mean you should only be good friends with people who tell you exactly what you want to hear? Of course not. You need friends who are honest with you.

But it is important to surround yourself with people who lift you up instead of drag you down. People who affirm your faith. We're not talking about a Christian bubble. But do spend a lot of time with people who fill you up with the goodness of God. Then go and fill others up with that same goodness. And out of the fullness of your faith and the encouragement of your closest relationships, you can serve and love unbelievers as Christ loved and served.

The Truth in Love

Wounds from a friend can be trusted,
but an enemy multiplies kisses.
PROVERBS 27:6 NIV

God-honoring relationships are those in which true
friends speak the truth in love to one another (Ephesians
4:15). People who, as Rachel Lynde from *Anne of Green
Gables* says, "pride themselves on speaking their mind," are
often proud of the fact that they "tell it like it is." While
this can be a refreshing change from well-meaning friends
who only tell you what you want to hear—and even
Christian friends who pretend everything is fine under
the guise of "keeping the peace"—Rachel Lynde is a good
example of someone who has forgotten to do so out of
love and is stuck on the pride part.

A true friend will go to another, many times in tears, knowing that the truth they need to say will be difficult and painful to hear, but they will go because God has called them to speak up. This is a "wound" that can be trusted. True friends do this out of love. True friends want to see one another be all that God intends for them to be. True friends don't want to see the other slip and fall.

If you ever feel prompted by God to talk to a friend who is going down a slippery path, make sure you are all prayed up. Ask God to go before you and prepare your friend's heart. Try to put yourself in her shoes and consider her feelings. Know that she may be offended, and it may take some time to heal the relationship. That's something you have to leave in God's hands.

If you are ever on the receiving end of such a conversation, respond with grace. Thank your friend for being honest with you, and know that the wound she has given you can be trusted. Pray with her, and ask her to hold you accountable for whatever the issue may be. Value her friendship forever. She is a keeper!

Choose Friends Wisely

*Don't befriend angry people or associate
with hot-tempered people, or you will learn
to be like them and endanger your soul.*
PROVERBS 22:24–25 NLT

142

Sometimes it's hard to find good friends. Maybe you've moved to a new city or state and you don't know anyone. Or maybe life has changed for you and you've outgrown your former friends by moving on to college or getting married or having a baby. Life can get lonely, and it's important to seek out good friendships wherever life finds you. God gives us clear direction about friendships so we can choose our friends wisely.

This proverb tells us not to be friends with angry people or those with hot tempers. You can tell a lot about a person by how they talk to others on the phone, how they talk about others to you, and how they talk to their children and husbands. Pay close attention. Don't get involved with women who are filled with bitterness and rage. This can eventually rub off on you if you spend too much time with them.

Instead, find a local Bible-believing church in your area and get involved. Go by yourself or with your husband and children. Find a way to serve, and get to know your fellow workers at church. Join a small group. Pray for open doors to meet new people. This is a great way to make friendships that will last for eternity.

Lord, thank You for Your friendship. You give the ultimate example of what friendship really is: laying down Your life for mine so that I might lay down my life for another. That's love. That's true friendship. Help me to be that kind of friend. Your Word tells me in John 15 that You call me friend! What an honor that You would choose me and love me unconditionally. I am a friend of God! So amazing! Let Your love shine through me always, and help me to bear fruit that will last in my friendships.

Heavenly Father, help me to surround myself with people who lift me up instead of drag me down. Give me wisdom so that I don't keep myself in a Christian bubble but choose my closest friends wisely. Please give me friends who love and honor You. Help me to be a good friend in return. Let our faith increase by our friendship so that we can encourage each other and serve You as You desire. Help me to speak the truth in love and to accept that truth graciously when it comes my way.

Lighten Up

A cheerful heart is good medicine,
but a crushed spirit dries up the bones.
PROVERBS 17:22 NIV

Can you think of a few friends that you find yourself "walking on eggshells" with frequently when it comes to certain subjects? Or maybe you have some things in your life that you are touchy about and have a hard time getting over? Missionary Amy Carmichael said: "If I take offence easily; if I am content to continue in cold unfriendliness, though friendship be possible, then I know nothing of Calvary love." Jesus said, "I have come that they may have life, and have it to the full" (John 10:10 NIV)!

Have a cheerful heart. Don't take yourself and your issues so seriously, because God is still on the throne, and He has ultimate control. Find the joy in the simple things of life. Don't worry about the little stuff. Don't make everything a big deal. John Maxwell says, "Get over yourself. Everyone else has."

And laugh! Multiple studies show that laughter can significantly reduce stress and in turn reduce chronic illness and disease. So laugh with your friends. Laugh hard. Laugh until you spray stuff out of your nose! It's good for your friendships and your stress level.

The bottom line is to lighten up. Enjoy the friendships God has given you.

Simple Gossip

*It is foolish to belittle one's neighbor; a sensible person
keeps quiet. A gossip goes around telling secrets, but
those who are trustworthy can keep a confidence.*
PROVERBS 11:12–13 NLT

If you have to glance at the door to see if anyone is
coming before you begin a conversation with someone,
you probably shouldn't be having that conversation! If that
thought bothers you even just a little, that's a pretty clear
sign that it's time to place a tighter rein on your tongue.

Keep the following scriptures as your guide:

Do not let any unwholesome talk come out
of your mouths, but only what is helpful for
building others up according to their needs,
that it may benefit those who listen.
EPHESIANS 4:29 NIV

Let your conversation be always full of
grace, seasoned with salt, so that you may
know how to answer everyone.
COLOSSIANS 4:6 NIV

This is a hard lesson to learn and an even harder action to put into practice. But you can stop yourself in your tracks if you need to. If you're in the middle of repeating something that isn't beneficial to anyone, stop yourself midsentence. Tell the person you are talking with that you shouldn't have said that and you are convicted of gossip. If the person understands and doesn't pressure you to tell the rest of the story—that is a true friend. If you do feel pressure, be firm about your conviction. Simple gossip is simply sinful. It hurts others, it ruins friendships, it is never harmless.

Stick to your guns and fasten your gums!

*Purity and Grace Attract
the Best Kind of Friends*

*One who loves a pure heart and who speaks
with grace will have the king for a friend.*
PROVERBS 22:11 NIV

If you have a pure heart and a pure conscience before God, you never have to watch your back. You don't have to be insecure in your relationships. You don't have to worry about what other people may be saying about you or what they might think of you. The way that you live your life is between you and God. If you are living a God-honoring life, you don't have to worry about the kind of friends you'll attract.

Having said that, it's important to remember that you cannot please everyone. People hated Jesus, so don't think that just because you're a Jesus-follower, everyone in your life will always be happy with you. Jesus upset a lot of people. He doesn't call us to please everyone—just Him! We need concern ourselves with pleasing only God and not worry about what everyone else thinks. The Proverbs are full of insight into what kind of wisdom we should be looking for, and it certainly doesn't come from everyone we know. God doesn't want you to be a people-pleaser, He wants you to be a Jesus-pleaser!

As you seek Jesus, the purity and grace you develop will attract the best kind of friends, the kind of friendships that honor God.

Promote Love

Whoever would foster love covers
over an offense, but whoever repeats
the matter separates close friends.
PROVERBS 17:9 NIV

Imagine this conversation: a friend tells you she heard that your mutual friend hurt your feelings. Your gut reaction may be to share the whole sob story and gain sympathy from your listener, thinking that's okay to do since you will end the conversation by saying that you are okay now and you've forgiven the offender. In fact, that's probably what most women do. But the Bible says to cover over that offense with love and don't repeat it. Instead, find a way to change the subject and let your friend know it's not something you think that you should repeat. Tell her that the matter has been—or is being—resolved and that you love them both. End of story. Responding in such a way promotes love and protects friendships. You are covering the friend who hurt you with love and grace.

Proverbs 17:17 (NIV) says: "A friend loves at all times, and a brother is born for a time of adversity." True friends will promote love at all times. Even when they don't fully understand what their friend is going through. Be that kind of friend. Ask God to help you develop these kinds of friendships. Ask Him to help you respond to friends out of love and to treat friends—and conversations with friends—like you would want to be treated and in the way you would like to be spoken of when you're not around.

Heavenly Father, please help me to have a cheerful heart! Let me be the friend who always has a smile on my face—not one of pretense but of a deep inner joy that comes from knowing You. Help me to always make room in my schedule for a friend in need. Help me to lighten up and not take offense easily. Forgive me of my pride that gets in the way so often. Show me how to put others before myself. Help me to promote love in my friendships and to protect them.

Forgive me for allowing simple gossip to happen in my friendships, dear Lord. I know it's wrong. Please help me to understand more fully how devastating the effects of gossip can be. I want my conversations to be full of love and grace. I want to build others up when I talk, and I don't want anyone to ever worry about what I might be saying about them when they aren't around. Help me to realize that You are listening in on every conversation. I want my words to honor You always.

You are more than the pain you've experienced.
God sees and feels your pain. No tear is
wasted. The Bible says He counts them.

KARY OBERBRUNNER

When Life Hurts

Full of Trouble

*LORD, you are the God who saves me; day and night
I cry out to you. May my prayer come before you; turn
your ear to my cry. I am overwhelmed with troubles
and my life draws near to death. . . . I call to you,
LORD, every day; I spread out my hands to you.*
PSALM 88:1–3, 9 NIV

Has there ever been a time in your life when you were begging God on a daily basis to do something? To change the plan. To bring some peace. To heal an illness. To bring a financial solution. Something. Anything. Can you relate to this psalm?

This psalmist, one of the sons of Korah, was at his lowest. The Bible says he was close to death. His soul was full of trouble. This psalm is an utterly honest prayer for God to show up. *Please, God, please! Do something! Help me! I'm asking the same thing every day. Please. Please.*

Does this sound like you?

Maybe your marriage is struggling. Maybe there is a serious illness in your family. Maybe you've lost a loved one and you are fighting off depression. Get real with God, and be honest with Him. Tell Him how you really feel. He can take it. He is close. He wants to hear from you. He wants to give you His peace in the midst of trouble.

If this doesn't sound like anything you've experienced yet in your life, you can probably think of at least one person who is experiencing trouble right now. Pray for them as you read through this section. Ask God to help you comfort them with His love.

A Good Reminder

It was you who split open the sea by your power;
you broke the heads of the monster in the waters.
It was you who crushed the heads of Leviathan
and gave it as food to the creatures of the desert.
PSALM 74:13–14 NIV

Some days we need a good reminder that God is still working in our lives. Maybe God seems distant and you cannot feel His presence. Or maybe trouble has found you, and you are overwhelmed with the stress of life. In this psalm, Asaph and his descendants needed help. They felt like God had forgotten them. But instead of giving up on Him, they decided to make a list of what God had already done. They reminded themselves of who God was and how He had already worked on their behalf. We would be wise to do the same.

Are you feeling as though God is far away? Do you wonder if He still cares about your personal struggles? The truth is that God is always aware of you and is constantly with you!

When you are tempted to doubt, speak truth into the moment. Repeat God's Word to your soul:

God will never leave nor forsake you. (Hebrews 13:5)
He is close to the brokenhearted. (Psalm 34:18)
He is not far from any of us. (Acts 17:27)

Make yourself a list of all the times you know for sure that God was there for you. Write down the blessings you have experienced. Take note of hardships you endured and lessons that God taught you. Then when you're tempted to doubt God's presence in your life, go back and remember how active He has been and how intimately He knows and cares about you.

Useful in His Hands

*Have mercy on me, my God, have mercy on me,
for in you I take refuge. I will take refuge in the shadow
of your wings until the disaster has passed. I cry out to
God Most High, to God, who vindicates me.*
PSALM 57:1–2 NIV

Do you ever wonder why bad things tend to happen to
you? Do you ever feel like you get more than your fair
share of problems to overcome at one time? Do you
believe more trials are sent your way than they are to
your friends? Oswald Chambers said: "If you are going
to be used by God, He will take you through a multitude
of experiences that are not meant for you at all, they are
meant to make you useful in His hands, and to enable you
to understand what transpires in other souls so that you
will never be surprised at what you come across."

The question then becomes, do you really want to be useful in His hands? This is serious business because being useful in His hands can hurt. Bad. There may be times that you feel literally used up and spit out. You may feel depleted and discouraged. You may feel betrayed and unwanted. But if you allow God to give you an eternal perspective and you begin to completely trust Him with your life, you will see His hand at work in mighty ways—even when life hurts.

If you truly want God to fulfill His purpose in you, allow yourself to be useful in His hands. He is faithful. Your pain will not be for nothing. God is at work in and through you. Trust Him.

Deep Distress

Be merciful to me, LORD, for I am in distress; my eyes grow weak with sorrow, my soul and my body with grief. My life is consumed by anguish and my years by groaning; my strength fails because of my affliction, and my bones grow weak.
PSALM 31:9–10 NIV

King David is credited as the author of many of the psalms. He experienced times of great blessing, but he also knew his share of deep suffering. And still he trusted God no matter what. You can see his great faith in verses such as Psalm 37:25 (NIV): "I was young and now I am old, yet I have never seen the righteous forsaken."

David's distress was caused by the poor choices he made (adultery, murder, lying) and the choices of those close to him (King Saul hunted him, his own son betrayed him). He feared for his life on many occasions, which caused him to cry out to God in sorrow and grief. Yet during that same psalm he was able to say: "Praise be to the LORD, for he showed me the wonders of his love" (Psalm 31:21 NIV).

When life hurts, are you able to look to God and say, "I praise You for Your love for me; I'm hurting but I trust You; I can't see past my grief, but I know You are faithful"?

Psalm 34:18 (NIV) says, "The LORD is close to the brokenhearted and saves those who are crushed in spirit." Jesus meets us in our distress. You may never feel closer to the Lord than you do when you are hurting. Reach out for Him. He is always reaching for you.

Father, these cries of David in the Psalms could be my very own. I feel just like this. My heart is troubled, and I need help. Why does it feel like You've rejected me, Lord? (Psalm 74:1). I'm having a hard time believing that You still care. But even still, I will remember who You are and what You have done for me. I trust that You will never leave me or forsake me. I trust that You are always working things out for my good. When I'm tempted to doubt Your presence in my life, help me to remember how faithful You have been in the past.

Jesus, thank You for promising to be close to the brokenhearted (Psalm 34:18). I'm not there right now, but I know someone who is. I ask that You would use me in her life. Open doors for me to be Your hands and feet in that situation. Help her to feel Your presence in her life, dear Lord. Use me in whatever way You want to. Thank You for preparing me to be Your vessel. Please give me Your eternal perspective and wisdom as I listen to Your promptings and follow after You.

Forgotten

O Lord, how long will you forget me? Forever?
How long will you look the other way? How long must
I struggle with anguish in my soul, with sorrow in my
heart every day? How long will my enemy have the
upper hand? Turn and answer me, O Lord my God!
Restore the sparkle to my eyes, or I will die.
PSALM 13:1–3 NLT

Do you ever feel forgotten? Like maybe your problems don't matter to God—or anyone at all?

David was the author of this psalm, and it is so refreshing to see his transparency throughout the Psalms as he prays to God. Yes, God is holy and awesome and powerful and majestic and able to do whatever He wants with anything in His creation. . .and yet He desires an intimate and honest relationship with each one of us! Incredible! Just like this psalm in which David pours out his heart to God and tells Him plainly how he feels, God wants us to come to Him with everything. All of our feelings, our anxieties, our fears, our hesitations, our frustrations, our hopes, our dreams, our nightmares— everything.

You can tell God when you feel forgotten. Don't feel guilty about doing so, thinking that God has enough problems to deal with. He cares about everything in your life. Even the little stuff.

During seasons of life where the sparkle has gone from your eyes and no one seems to care, remember that you have not been forgotten. God sees you and has a plan at work in your life right at this very moment.

Disappointment

Many are the plans in a person's heart,
but it is the LORD's purpose that prevails.
PROVERBS 19:21 NIV

Dealing with the disappointments of life can be hard on the soul and the body. Medical studies clearly show that stress and anxiety can lead to major health problems. So how can a person continue to deal with disappointment and not let the stress get to her?

You stop being a control freak. You make plans, but you quit trying to control the outcome. You leave things in God's hands. You relax because you know that God is in control. You memorize the following verses and repeat them often, trusting that God's Word is full of living power (Hebrews 4:12):

Don't worry about anything; instead, pray
about everything. Tell God what you need, and
thank him for all he has done. Then you will
experience God's peace, which exceeds anything we
can understand. His peace will guard your hearts
and minds as you live in Christ Jesus.
PHILIPPIANS 4:6–7 NLT

Cast all your anxiety on
him because he cares for you.
1 PETER 5:7 NIV

"For I know the plans I have for you," declares the
LORD, "plans to prosper you and not to harm you,
plans to give you hope and a future."
JEREMIAH 29:11 NIV

Today's proverb reminds us that it's okay to plan, so
go ahead. But remember that the Lord's purpose *always*
prevails. If your plan does not align with God's, it is
meaningless. If you make a plan without seeking God
first, don't be disappointed when it fails—that's a given.
Instead, take your plans straight to God. There will still
be bumps and disappointments along the path for
the Christian—that's also a given—but
God promises to be with you.

Failure

Whom have I in heaven but you? And there is nothing on earth that I desire besides you. My flesh and my heart may fail, but God is the strength of my heart and my portion forever.
PSALM 73:25–26 ESV

You can probably relate to what the psalmist is saying in these verses: *You know what? I've done everything poorly. I've messed up big-time. I failed. There is nothing I can do to fix it.*

You're right. There is nothing you can do to fix it. But Jesus *can*. He already did! Jesus has conquered sin and death. He has covered over all of our failures. "Because you are my helper, I sing for joy in the shadow of your wings. I cling to you; your strong right hand holds me securely" (Psalm 63:7–8 NLT). When we fail, we sometimes want to run and hide like a shy child who hides herself in her mother's skirt. We're embarrassed, and the failure plays over and over again in our heads like a movie.

Here's the deal: It's okay to run and hide for a while. We can safely cling to Jesus. We can hide ourselves in Him. He will restore us in His timing (1 Peter 5:9–11). He will change our perspective and attitude about our failure if we let Him.

In John Maxwell's book *Failing Forward*, he says: "No matter what you've experienced, remember this: There are people who've had it better than you and done worse. And there are people who've had it worse than you and done better. . . . Past hurts can make you bitter or better—the choice is yours."

God Is Awake

I lift up my eyes to the mountains—where does my help come from? My help comes from the LORD, the Maker of heaven and earth. He will not let your foot slip—he who watches over you will not slumber.
PSALM 121:1–3 NIV

Where has God been through all of this? you may ask. *It's been hard. Too hard. How could He let any of this happen?*

Philip Yancey, in *Where Is God When It Hurts?*, wrote: "He has been there from the beginning. . . . He has joined us. He has hurt and bled and cried and suffered. He has dignified for all time those who suffer, by sharing their pain. He is with us now, ministering to us through his Spirit."

In Luke 12:32 (NIV), after telling us how useless it is to worry, Jesus says, "Do not be afraid, little flock, for your Father has been pleased to give you the kingdom." Can't you hear and feel the love in God's heart for you? When life hurts, give it to Jesus. In Matthew 11:28 (NLT) He says: "Come to me, all of you who are weary and carry heavy burdens, and I will give you rest." *REST!* How we need rest.

"Don't be afraid, little one. I'm here. I want to take your burden. I want to give you rest."

So as Victor Hugo aptly put it, "Have courage for the great sorrows in life, and patience for the small ones. And when you have laboriously accomplished your daily tasks, go to sleep in peace, God is awake."

Father, thank You for the prayers of Your people in the Psalms. They give me a great example of how You want me to come to You in prayer with honesty and humility. Thank You for caring about my smallest need. I'm going to trust that You haven't forgotten me in times of difficulty and great distress. My heart is weary, and my body is feeling the effects. Give me strength to keep on. I want to trust You. I want to live for You. Continue to breathe new life and hope into my life. I love You, O Lord, my strength.

I've messed up, Lord. Pretty big. And I'm disappointed and scared. I feel like such a failure. How can this be fixed? Please show up, God. Please! I need help. I've made such a mess of things. I didn't come to You first, and I set off on my own path, thinking that I knew best. And now look what I've done. Will You step in? Will You turn things around? I'm so sorry. I cannot fix this without You. Help me to move forward, trusting that You have everything under control and that You can redeem the mess I've made.

Expect to have hope rekindled.
Expect your prayers to be answered
in wondrous ways. The dry seasons in life
do not last. The spring rains will come again.

SARA BAN BREATHNACH

Joy in the Morning

Confidence in His Goodness

I remain confident of this: I will see the goodness of the LORD in the land of the living.
PSALM 27:13 NIV

You may not understand any of the reasons for the pain that you've experienced in this life. Maybe some of it was because of your own poor choices or the choices of those closest to you. Maybe it just doesn't make any sense at all. No matter what has happened, know this: Jesus wants to wrap His arms around you and show you His goodness. He is calling you back to the safety and protection of His love.

Oswald Chambers said: "We never realize at the time what God is putting us through; we go through it more or less misunderstandingly; then we come to a luminous place, and say—'Why, God has girded me, though I did not know it!'"

God has a plan. He will use it. Whatever you've gone through, God is working. He hasn't forgotten you. He is preparing you for His purposes. You can have total confidence in His goodness.

Though you may have experienced unbelievable difficulty, it won't last. A new season is coming. You will see the goodness of God in the land of the living!

As Psalm 30:5 (NLT) says, "Weeping may last through the night, but joy comes with the morning."

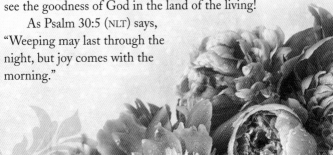

Joy in Your Presence

You make known to me the path of life;
you will fill me with joy in your presence,
with eternal pleasures at your right hand.
PSALM 16:11 NIV

When we've gone through times of great pain and difficulty in our lives, we have quite literally shared in Christ's sufferings.

Consider these verses:

Now if we are children, then we are heirs—
heirs of God and co-heirs with Christ,
if indeed we share in his sufferings in order
that we may also share in his glory.
ROMANS 8:17 NIV

Dear friends, do not be surprised at the fiery ordeal that has come on you to test you, as though something strange were happening to you. But rejoice inasmuch as you participate in the sufferings of Christ, so that you may be overjoyed when his glory is revealed.
1 PETER 4:12–13 NIV

Sharing in the sufferings of Christ is a powerful thing. The late youth speaker Dave Busby said, "The end of your rope is God's permanent address." We can find Christ in the suffering, and He will give us joy in His presence. He has made known to us the path to eternal life through Jesus!

He promises to fill us with His joy—and we don't have to wait until heaven for that. We have access to His peace, joy, grace, and presence right now while we live on earth, through the power of the Holy Spirit (Philippians 4:7; Hebrews 4:16).

Be greatly encouraged by Romans 15:13 (NIV): "May the God of hope fill you with all joy and peace as you trust in him, so that you may overflow with hope by the power of the Holy Spirit."

Better Times

Many people say, "Who will show us better times?"
Let your face smile on us, Lord. You have given me
greater joy than those who have abundant harvests of
grain and new wine. In peace I will lie down and sleep,
for you alone, O Lord, will keep me safe.

PSALM 4:6–8 NLT

In the book *Anne of Green Gables* by Lucy Maud Montgomery, Anne and Marilla are discussing Anne's disappointment at a recent occurrence. Anne says, "I can't help flying up on the wings of anticipation. It's as glorious as soaring through a sunset, almost pays for the thud." But Marilla replies, "Well, maybe it does. But I'd rather walk calmly along and do without flying and thud."

In this fallen world, there will always be flying and thud. Max Lucado says to *"lower your expectations of earth. This isn't heaven, so don't expect it to be."* Remember, don't be surprised that life can be nasty here (1 Peter 4:12), but don't despair either. Better times are ahead.

In Joel 2:25 (ESV), God says to the people of Judah: "I will restore to you the years that the swarming locust has eaten." He promises that all who call on the name of the Lord will be saved (Joel 2:32), and He reminds the people of His goodness: "Return to the Lord your God, for he is gracious and compassionate, slow to anger and abounding in love, and he relents from sending calamity" (Joel 2:13 NIV).

If you've gone through difficult times, ask God to restore those years. Ask Him to use those life lessons to further His kingdom here and make you more like Christ. And always remember that a perfect heaven is awaiting you if you have trusted Christ as your Savior (John 14:1–4).

Heavenly Father, help me to find You in the sufferings of life. Help me not to be surprised when I experience trouble here in this messed-up world. Help me to lower my expectations of earth without falling into despair. Please give me Your joy and Your peace for every moment here on earth. Thank You for the promise of eternal life that I can constantly hope for and look forward to! Please restore the years that the locusts have eaten in my life. Use them to further Your kingdom and conform me to Your image.

Father, I trust that I will see Your goodness here and now as I go through life on earth. My greatest joy is knowing You and living for You. You have forgiven me so much—help me to love much. You have removed the weight of sin and stress from my shoulders and have turned my cries into a dance. You have removed my sins as far as the east is from the west. You have given me freedom and a clear conscience. Thank You, Jesus! Fill me with joy in Your presence all the days of my life.

The Greatest Joy

The LORD is compassionate and gracious, slow to anger, abounding in love. He will not always accuse, nor will he harbor his anger forever; he does not treat us as our sins deserve or repay us according to our iniquities. For as high as the heavens are above the earth, so great is his love for those who fear him; as far as the east is from the west, so far has he removed our transgressions from us. As a father has compassion on his children, so the LORD has compassion on those who fear him.

PSALM 103:8–13 NIV

This psalm is a balm to the hardened soul. God doesn't treat us as our sins deserve. He is compassionate. He is gracious. Because of Jesus' work on the cross, He's not angry with us! Instead, He is abounding in love. He sees us as Jesus sees us: *paid for!* Our sins have been obliterated.

J. I. Packer said: "There is, however, equally great incentive to worship and love God in the thought that, for some unfathomable reason, He wants me as His friend, and desires to be my friend, and has given His Son to die for me in order to realize this purpose."

No matter how many times you've messed up, God loves you and desires to be your friend. We have the greatest joy in knowing that because of Jesus, God doesn't hold our sins against us. We are free and dearly loved.

Thanks Forever

You turned my wailing into dancing;
you removed my sackcloth and clothed me
with joy, that my heart may sing your
praises and not be silent. LORD my God,
I will praise you forever.
PSALM 30:11–12 NIV

In Luke 7:36–50, the Bible tells us of a sinful woman who broke protocol and went into the house of a Pharisee to anoint Jesus' feet with oil. The Pharisees were disgusted that Jesus let this sinful woman touch him. But Jesus said in verse 47 (NIV): "Therefore, I tell you, her many sins have been forgiven—as her great love has shown. But whoever has been forgiven little loves little."

Like this sinful woman, we've been forgiven much. And we continue to need grace and forgiveness on a daily basis—sometimes on a moment-by-moment basis. Jesus took care of all of that for us on the cross. He paid for our past, present, and future sins. C. S. Lewis said: "Christ died for men precisely because men are not worth dying for; to make them worth it." Jesus made us worth dying for. We don't understand it, we don't know why He loves us—but He chooses to. He offers us a completely clear conscience. He turns our cries into a dance, and now we can sing and give Him thanks. As Christ-followers, we can live out our short time on earth with joy and hopeful expectation!

And just as Jesus said to the sinful woman, he says the same to us: "Your faith has saved you; go in peace" (Luke 7:50 NIV).

"Lord my God, I will praise you forever."